kin

kin

poems by

Crystal Williams

Michigan State University Press
East Lansing

∞ The paper used in this publication meets the minimum requirements of
ANSI/NISO Z39.48–1992 (R 1997) (Permanence of Paper).

Michigan State University Press
East Lansing, Michigan 48823-5202

Printed and bound in the United States of America.

04 03 02 01 00   1 2 3 4 5 6 7 8 9

Library of Congress Cataloging-in-Publication Data
Williams, Crystal, 1970-
    kin : poems / by Crystal Williams.
        p.   cm.
    ISBN 0-87013-548-1
  1. Interracial marriage—United States—Poetry. 2. Adoptees—United
States—Poetry. 3. Family—United States—Poetry. 4. Afro-American
women—Poetry. I. Title.
    PS3573. I448414 K56 2000
    811' .54—dc21   99-050564

Cover design by Ariana Grabec-Dingman
Book design by Nicolette Rose

Visit Michigan State University Press on the World-Wide Web at:
www.msu.edu/unit/msupress

In honor of my parents

Pinkney and Mo

no matter
and because.

"I am not an earth nor an adjunct of an earth,
I am the mate and companion of people,
all just as immortal and fathomless as myself..."

Walt Whitman—"Song of Myself"

"I've stayed in the front yard all my life.
I want to peek at the back
Where it's rough and untended and hungry weed grows.
A girl gets sick of a rose."

Gwendolyn Brooks—"A Song in the Front Yard"

Contents

Oo-bop-she-bam

Acknowledgments:

The following poems or versions of these poems have appeared in:
A Gathering of the Tribes ("Once Upon A Time"); *African Voices* ("Collard Folk"); *Beyond the Frontier* ("In Search of Aunt Jemima"); *Catch the Fire: A Cross-Generational Anthology of African American Poets* ("In Search of Aunt Jemima"); *Icarus* ("In Search of Aunt Jemima," "Prayer," "At 25 I Have Already Begun To Like Lou Rawls," "Zawadi," and "As On Every Saturday at 12."); *Salonika* ("Collard Folk" and "Prayer" which appeared as "Joy"); *The Madison Review* ("It Wasn't Not Funny" and "Refrigerator Mouth"); *The Red Brick Review* ("Dré"); *Pandora* ("Johnny"); *WV* ("Dreadlock"); and "In Search of Aunt Jemima" appeared in *Poetry Nation: the North American Anthology of Fusion Poetry*, edited by Regie Cabico and Todd Swift, published by Vehicule Press.

The following people deserve my gratitude:
Robert Gumbleton for the walrus; Mary Dorothy Payette for the lessons in having soup; the McGrath's for your sweet songs; Marilyn "Murl" McCormick—for everything and forever; Freida Gorrecht and Virginia Crowthers for brushing off the bruises; Kenneth Carroll for generosity; Mrs. A. Leach for lunch; and Dr. Olive Taylor for context.

For their support of and advice on the compilation of this manuscript:
Gabrielle Civil, Poppy, Kenneth A. McClane.

For their generous encouragement:
Martha Ann Bates, Ruth Danon, Jennifer Egan, Susanna Kaysen, James Lineville, M. Mark, Georgia A. Popoff, and Karen Volkman.

For their friendship, love to:
Barry Abrams, Skip Baker, Ava Chin, E. Catherine Falvey (and Anna Laura Grace), Daryl Garrett, Cheryll Y. Greene (and Kamali), Marie King, Rosamond King, Paula Kennedy, Steven Klym, Anne Larsen, Jennifer Lee, JoAnn McGreevy, Betty Miller, Benjamin Muhammad (and Shakirah), Michael and Claire Neal, James Nevius, and Robyn M. Turner.

Additional thanks to: my cohorts at the NYU Book Centers, The Province-town Fine Arts Work Center, The Women's Auxilary (Aunt May, Aunt Lynn, Leona, Vicki, and Sandi), Steve Canon, Keith Roach for the ongoing nudge, Bob Holman, all the performance poets (write on!), The Nuyorican Poets Café for providing such an essential forum, and

wherever you are, whoever you are,
to my biological family,
for having a faith big enough to let me go . . .

rhythm

For The Woman Who Didn't Know My Name

In some old men there is a softness
in voice a hint of dust y Alabama
summers of boyhood & the swagger
of their walk whispers of past
glories when their hips carried more
than bone & their torsos fattened ribs
& their feet them as small boys in play
around the spot in town where men once herded
my people. There were those games too.

In old men there are wrinkles perfectly placed where drops
of food & spittle settle. And they'll whisper of spat
tobacco   of dogs   of whips   in tongues   to their sons & girl
children & they to their sons & girl children.

music: one

The Famous Door

Be-Bop, De-Bop, Be-Bop
smooooooooth like sass
n jazz n momma-n-mary
at the bar n you singin "Route 66."

You, on the sneak, askin
momma on a date n the cops followin
momma-n-mary home 'cause white
girls didn't hang out in (black) jazz bars
in 1966. Hell, proper white
girls probably didn't hang t'all.

N you at the ivory-n-ebony
crooning "I Left My Heart . . ." to momma,
winkin n smilin n jazzin n profilin
n sangin n sangin
n sangin n soundin
sweeeeeeeeeeeeeeee   t.

Prayer

for Richard Pinkney Williams 1907–1981

You were jazz and leather on a rainy day,
soft and pliable, aged to perfection with wrinkles of little modesty,
deep and giving of themselves.

My little hands seemed ridiculous
as they traced lines relaying all the past laughs
which bellowed from The Good Place,
full of music, for only me.

You were bicycle rides to the park, Kentucky Fried Chicken
everyday after kindergarten, Slip-n-Slide on birthdays, secret
sips of beer, songs sung, Alabama skins on my knee.

Were washing backs, Ivory soap,
dirty bath water; golf clubs and Palmer Woods, the universe
around which I ran and skated and danced and swam
coming always back to you, breathless,
expectant of the everything and nothing in particular
only you could give.
I was your girl.

You were sickness, seizure, and old—a too worn leather,
brittle with bruises placed there long ago only now, visible
and hindering and ugly. You were no speech
no movement 'cept slow and deliberate.
Tired and gray, you became a stranger whose eyes
shone, then only if moon/sun/zodiac/weather permitted.
You were Sick. Seizure. Dead. Gone. Anger.

Long ago,
when I was your girl
when our house was yellow brick
and Halloween was the scariest thing to me;
long ago, before I knew
of money, jobs, sadness, or loss, I knew you
Daddy, and Joy.

The Masked Woman

Momma is a big-boned woman, stands five-nine
with a head full of used-to-be auburn hair. Black Irish.
Years ago she wore a conservative bun. When loose it shimmied
like oil, was dense as swamp marsh, was the extent of her
extravagance.

After her mother died she cared for the brothers, worked
herself through school, married Daddy. *I just loved him.*
Race didn't enter the equation, only age.
She weighed the 30-year-fault & concluded
she loved him enough to lose him.

I have questioned her trying to
ferret out some rabble-rousing. She was too old
to be a hippie. Still, some act must account for us.
Political? No, I wasn't political.

At five when I asked, "When will the dirt wash off my skin?"
she searched out the best public school in Detroit.
Of Roper City & Country Day I remember only
how white the children were,
the bubbled domes of classrooms, saying goodbye
to no one in particular.

This photo was taken in Alabama, Daddy's folks surrounding us,
their black skins withered. Their storied music is lost to me.
I was too young. Just a bright Black
baby under a southern sky, extending Momma's hip.

When I ask why the Afro wig & Curtis Mayfield sunglasses,
she sighs sweet breath on my face,

That's just how it was. I didn't always
wear it. In the car . . . well . . .

silence and memory snatch at her eyes

. . . down there, Daddy drove up front
& I rode in back with you, hidden.

This is all she'll say. I take it greedily.

When friends see the photo, colored folk
flanking a light-skinned Cleopatra Jones.
"Who's that pretty, light-skinned lady
holding you?" they ask.

My mother.
She's my mother, I say. Isn't she striking.

At 25, I Have Already Begun to Like Lou Rawls

When I die
you will find all my socks light blue,
my pants bright green, my shoes nothing
memorable, and you will describe me as
having been daringly free
of fashion.

Even now my disinterest in scarves can be viewed as eccentric.

When I die
my manicured hands,
which have always been plump
and found keyboards necessary,
will have a fine layer of dirt under their nails,
and will be known for their slow and gentle touch.

I have planted cosmos, asters.

And, you'll remember the drag of my hips
swaying with only necessary movement.
When I die
I will have just then, emerged.
Completed at last, having added few originalities.

This is your legacy.

When I die,
I will wear
the face of my mother,
gladly.

Yea, Though I Walk . . .

Yesterday, I stood naked
Except for a barrette—gold
And tarnishing at

The edges—in the mirror.
How is it that when days are long,
Obscure, and flee my grip, I
Understand only that
Glass and dust gather?
How is it that when my cat hides herself

In closets as if her bones

Will fall apart, recompose themselves
And dance her into something else, I
Liken those days to you? Mother, the
Kitchen is perpetually dirty,

The bathroom filled with lint balls, the
House in disrepair. I
Revolve able to only, finally, sit naked
On the couch. So
Unlike you who would clean and

Grub until your hands were raw.
How unlike you I am in

These most mundane matters.
How dissimilar we are in
Everything visible. I

Vacillate over sitcoms
And books, seldom question
Luxuries/necessities like cabs or expensive
Linens. Yet, my
Eyes, brown and wide, reflect
Your name.

On days, when I am confused,
Fretting, or

Decided, I see your green/gray
Eyes peering back through the dust
And am quieted.
To outsiders, our skins different as this day.
Here, though, where the pounding is soft as your hand on my cheek, no.
    Salvation/sameness grows in soft hushed tones, like flutters, like wings.

Order of Adoption in the Matter of Minor #44478

for Altheia? Moore?

At four days old, light brown and borrowed,
like sugar from a neighbor,
they opened their door and drew me

in. Wrapped their arms around the smile
momma says has always been larger than the Joe
Louis Arena and taught me to walk,
my wings becoming shoes, Easter
bonnets, pink Huffy's.

Woman, do your arms get cold and concave
with the coming of September 26th?
Did the other six children, their brown eyes
longing, look just over your shoulder
to the clear sky? Have they asked my name?
Surely they have asked my name . . .

Have you imagined
me?
How
have you imagined
me?

14

I will tell you
my hips are rounded and wide
my nails grow askew
my hair is fine and abundant
my eyes are alert.
I am happy

I am known as:
Marilyn-Theresa,
Richard-Pinkney,
Crystal-Ann
Williams.

music: two

Rites of Passage

for Harold Neal

Would you remember an imposing man with little to no gleam in his eye,
seriously tall and narrow, who reminded you of all the jive hip cool
jazz men (side swept tam included)
your father brought to the house
whose language was the richness being Black required
in the time and place they learned to be
bop?

Would you recall his gaze as it revealed your most
unadorned self, made you feel
a specimen.

Surely you would wonder how time had settled on him;
what mischief he was causing; for whom he was making things unpleasant.

During the years you found no beauty in the mirror
you'd invoke, with fondness, that day. In fact, would replay
the scene in which you were surrounded by sun/wind/pavement,
hiding behind the shoulder of your friend, as his father, the man with
the Black Bottom eyes said dryly,
"You are a beautiful young lady."

You would revisit those words; would struggle with them, pulling
and tugging, understanding, misunderstanding, until finally,
time allowed that—if nothing else—a compliment should be
accepted/acknowledged with grace,
as somehow (with uncharacteristic meekness)
you think you did.

Poem for My Sisters

Rob, just out of prison, caught my scent
while I was on that gig where I'd mastered the direct ambush,
selling sucker's faces on muscled bodies, wanted posters, anything
they weren't. An American phenomenon, I've decided.
His hollow eyes scavenged the curves I'd gained by shedding.

I wanted chicken. He insisted on steak.
I wanted Diet Coke. He ordered wine.
I wanted no dessert. He made me eat pie.

That summer I learned to
use an answering machine offensively,
be thankful for intuition, he didn't know where I lived,
grow eyes in the back of my head.

And I learned to curse his name
for making me, at that table, on that night,
feel like only a woman
and his eyes,
which made me feel like the woman I wanted to be,
fleeting as it was.

A,
_____

*(I am so hungry for you my stomach
bloats and I am the glazed eyes of starvation.)*

Listened for you, saw movement on tv,
inhaled ten chickens, eight pizzas, six
pounds of grain, gulped down
this nocallnocallnocall until
my stomach bloated.

Could be I came on too subtly.
I take back everything I didn't
say, hear? I take it all back, hunch over,
dig my nails into the earth, raise,
dust blowing from my arms—
a pregnant-lipped lumberjack-woman
with arms full of all I've taken back.

Squeaked when you wanted squawk.
I am a lion. I am an elephant. I am a two
hundred voice gospel choir—with glazed eyes.

Could be tomorrow, if I rise into
sanity, I'll inhale two less pizzas,
one less pound of grain.

Could be the day after, if I rise into
sanity, I will not flick the channel, will
search the tearful eyes of Zaire—an absurd mirror
of starvation.

In preparation, I've begun gathering
the fragments of your name
from the broken windows and
bloodied ears of my neighbors.

I gather and gorge. I am gathering
and gorging.

Hey A,

(Mr. Sausage Lips)
for Daryl Francine Garrett

so when your lips slathered
& then stuck to my neck
like maple syrup & butta
greasin me all up
wuz that like some fat man
sneakin a second plate
when he ain't done wit the first?

& when u floated them soft
sweeter-n-a-buttermilk-biscuit-dipped-in-honey
words my way

what wuz u offerin?

cuz, just days later
like some rude Thanksgiving guest
u up & said, "I'm full
so no thankya, kindly, ma'am"

tell ya what:
don't be sneakin seconds
when u ain't done wit the first
don't be offerin biscuits
to folk who ain't hungry &
keep them sausage lips
on your face & offa my neck.

Johnny

Mother says, eyes traveling off,
when we were very little
she bathed us in that umber
seventies sink—naked and brown and soft is
how long we been knowin each other.

There were closets full of fingers
touching our wet places—you and I, Brother-Neighbor.
And climbed fences, juice and cookies. It was us
there, our world small and round
enough for our hands to carry.

Years after my family moved
mother told stories: of the swing
as you walked into it,
something, a year younger,
I would never have allowed.
Your eyes, she said, in another world,
"Well, he's not as bright as you . . . "

My eyes travel over faces
and behind them, searching.
Interest is beauty. I've tried to tell
her of the burden.

Johnny, when clothes found our eyes and we saw
what could be behind them; when
our tongues no longer spoke the soft talk; when
we grew into me licking my chapped lips,
you scraping residue from your hands,
we became adults.

We have become adults.
I visit Detroit and cannot stand
the sound of Aretha's voice
wrapping around your name.

Dreadlock

Saw you Dread.

On the first night
even though I perm my hair
& smoke way too much, in your absence,
jumped the broom with you anyway,
had two-point-five warrior-dreadlocked babies,
a dog named Mojo & a cat named Jubilee.

On the second night
saw you with a little white girl.
She was real small and pretty with dyed-
permed hair & a cigarette in her left hand.
You were earlobes & lips & syrupy sweetness

Saw you.
Dread.

Exercise in Tension or Truth or Whatever

7:45 and 96 degrees, the breeze crosses
between the blue-shoe-woman and the man
in pants so white he is a just fallen snow.

Five minutes to docking we become a conglomerate,
demanding our buses, houses, beds.

Hot pink and black stripes ride over the buttocks of Girl.
Between middle and right is a sticky looking man.
His robot rendition of "The Entertainer," obscene.
Emanating from some obscured place is the distracted
whistle that has imploded my ear drums for the last half hour.

I wanna snatch it away. I wanna tell the fat
man with stupid eyes to stop slurping his water
between the hairs at the nap of my neck. I wanna whisper
to Girl that fashion is elusive and Poly & Ester are The Man.

Instead I still. Wait for the boat to dock,
wonder if the wind will take with it the smell of my
"It breaks my heart when you do that" cigarette.

29

I begin my march towards a waiting,
see-you-twice-a-year-mother who is beginning
her second week—in a series of four. She will expect
to be kissed, asked how her day has unfolded.
The cigarette I stuff back into its box.

"The Cholesterol Can Make You Stupid..."

Momma

Last night me and Momma whispered
as if I were five again.

Uncle is forgetful. His speech,
although still funny, is slurred, like Daddy's.
Momma has just noticed this. I knew it right off.
But that's how things work when you don't see
someone for ten odd years.

Yesterday, Uncle walked into the closet, came out,
face reddening with a laugh, said, "Oh,"
mumbled about progress.

It worried Momma.
Closets are restrictive and
depending on what kind of motion you desire,
appropriate. We've bought tons of oatmeal.
Momma says his cholesterol is too high and his brain
is not getting enough oxygen.
I want to ask her
whose is?

Collard Folk

(for the Women's Auxiliary)

Mudia Pearl at stove front
wrist on hip, wooden hand stirrin
pots. Children runnin, cryin, laughin,
gettin whoopin's and yelled at bout
home trainin which Great Granddaddy Verdell
say we ain't got. Momma calls to us bout behavioral
modifications & what-nots.

Uncle Ruff & Delmar & Granddaddy
shootin shit in corner side, chompin they bits
over cream-corn smellin corn bread.

Aunt Mame, cousin Reve, Mama & Cecil playin Bidwhist.
Momma say Uncle Cecil can't play worth a horse's ass,
can't shoot shit, & always been a bit funny like that.

Ham's done. Cornbread's keepin warm. Turkey been out.
Lil-big John keeps gettin his hand slapped
for stealin frostin from Bertha's cake.

Everybody's waiting on them Collard Greens.

Collards, this time, was a bit tart.
So, Mudia stirs vinegar to cut, sugar
to sweetin vinegar's cut, seasonin to flavor.

Clifton and Daisy is back from they Kool-Aid trip,
is all kissy-kissy & didn't fool nobody.
Mudia cursin & yellin at us children.
Momma reach for me to re-braid my hair.

"Momma, why we always gotta wait
on them Collard Greens?" She say,
"Remy, to get good collards,
ya gotta add a little of this,
stir in a little of that, put some love into &
some other what-nots, let it do what it's got to do
& in the end you'll see
that when you work with what you got,
you'll get what you want."

dance

Dré

Tonight, when the Cabbie (who had a jones for death)
sped past the orange and brown blur of Pay Less Shoes,
hunting New York potholes, my discman skipped: *I'll hasten*
to His throne, I'll hasten to His throne, I'll hasten to His throne.
Which reminded me of the third to last time I saw you,
helping somebody's hymn-humming Grandmamma
try on nine dollar shoes in the self-serve Pay Less Shoes.

Was reminded of Sistah Milicent's lopsided hobble and staccato:
"Sistah, be nicer to the Bruthas, they don't know
what to make of you. You're scaring them off."
To which you responded, "Bullshit!" (although, never to her face.)
Was reminded of the play we produced, how bad an actor you were.

The point is:
When Angie called whispering—
I didn't go to D.C.
I didn't see you off.

It's just that when I pass by any Pay Less,
see a young brother with vampire eyes reading Les Brown,
glimpse "Come join us in the fight!" or hear a certain contentedness
I hear: *When it's nowhere to go I know I can go to Him . . .*
and the purple-blue sky is full with you.

The questions creep, Dré, like a New York-mugger-smog,
slow and disarming until I am stopped in mid-thought,
am aware of you in whatever day-to-day thing I was doing,
and cannot breathe.

I know in the end
it doesn't matter how
you got it, when you had it, if our fluids ever exchanged
from your wet and slippery greetings on my cheek.

It doesn't matter if you were,
if you weren't, if you were both.
I do admit to sometimes wondering
what were your reasons for not telling
and, did you hasten?

Dré, I pray you hastened.

Benjamin

Beyond the bathroom
before you reach the stair
is The Door. Beyond that—
your bedroom where you want to go
rest yourself, lay lash to lash.

In sleep, you've learned,
the dead only sigh. Her breath
is the chicken wings and barbecue sauce
of your sisters sweet sixteen.
You are a vegetarian.

So, you set your jaw
and step—a baby teetering—into the jerking
and rattling of your bones. This ghost mutates,

is an invisible linebacker,
tuff as shit and enveloping as the
dirt you played in as a child.

39

This ghost is harder to
shake than a prison-yard vendetta,
her nails long shivs. Your back has bled
for two years and two months.
Your face is marked with

four bone white scars
and you are Maasai.

The Prospect of Tomi-Terre
(1980–1998)

Perhaps if I told you she was the one
whose hair, after years of expression
finally settled into a whispering bob,
who begged nurtured pardons,
who'd extend her forearm at crosswalks.
If I explained hers would have been the brown-eyed boy
dancing beneath clothes racks until Gerber jingles
roused a forgotten sentiment,

perhaps then.
Or maybe

I should tell
how dark alleys can be,
how brick echoes. Her name
nefarious on his breath. Her name
pushing from their questioning eyes.

Grab onto her quickly
before knives shred our faith like lettuce,
or a Black girl's skin. Breath deep. Don't ponder
the smallness of trunks, the thickened blood shifting his eyes.

Stay with things known: the Grand Canyon smile,
the soda-pop with pizza sass, The Dream
ripening and peach cobbler and family
reunions. Tomi-Terre should be here.

Not in that alley, in that trunk
and not in the dark
and not being searched
and not being stabbed
and not lost, gone,
and not lost.
And not gone.

Curating the Boogie Down

*"Don't push me 'cause I'm close to the edge, I'm trying not to lose my head, uh-huh huh huh huh.
It's like a jungle sometimes, it makes me wonder how I keep from going under..."*

Grand Master Flash and The Furious Five

Here we are:
you like some janet jackson video extra
all ghetto-chic'd out
in the "damn, this ain't what I thought it'd be,"
Boogie-Down Bronx & me like Morticia Adams,
butt muscles clenched, recoiling at

Dollar-stores where five bones
buys three things, Hip-hop
outlets, countries of security guards.
All for a neon-green rubber-bottomed
New York Citay bookbag.

& you, "daaamn, peep this shit!
. . . what's wrong witchu?"

My chest is exploding
into a double-headed dragon,
the flame in my mouth is a giant
pissed-off tarantula.

Ain't no curtis-blow ghost
dipping his mike in gold 'round here.
Ain't no memorialized adidas swinging
from sign-posts. Ain't no break
dancers. Hell, Run hot-footed to God,
married a tenderoni, & lives
in a condo downtown. The Sugar Hill
Gang jetted back to Jersey like a scud.

Fifteen years ago a little girl was expunged
on this corner. Some idiot was shooting
at some other idiot who tagged the wrong wall,
a bullet found her seven-year-old body convenient.

Here. This corner. & the sound of her
pulsing will not will not WILL NOT. STOP. SCREAMING.

Tour Guiding Our Nation's Capital

Stretched polyester
blue skirt & white
oxford with mic in hand,
pointing towards the dead
politicians' monuments. Voice

instructing the slurpee
instamatic disposable camera
holders, the stretch-smile wearers,
the high-pitch not-a-worry-in-the-worlders
to turn & behold

the greatness

whizzing beside them. The things you know,
like the five hundred, fifty-five foot, five
& one eighth inch white penis protruding from the grass,
are jewels. You, among the treasures

will fall from them quick as
cherry blossoms or that black
tag on your chest, nameless & glaring.

Sunday Dinner at Miss Rayella's

South Carolina is caught in your throat. We gather
between a lulling bass & the staccato of things unsaid,

around the mahogany of your Sunday table. Your children
live in the warm-wet place just beneath your tongue.

    A full-grown & simmering son,

his world thirteen by fourteen, one hundred & eighty two square feet
of instant replay: what he should have done.

    A ripe & denying daughter,

her voice heavy with both Columbia's,
full of accusation.

    & you, with loaded plate,

push & pass between us, exist in the doorjamb
between his madness & your guilt.

    & you, with checkbook full
of never-good-enough-day-worker money,
are rent & car repair & whim.

The quiet has amassed in the crevices of your pantry.

Our migration quiets your moaning eyes.
When all is ready we will

    hush,

gather like antiqued pinched lace, burgeon with silence more noble
than our psalms & muted amens, will consider,

with each pass of the bowl, how it would be to cast off these refrains
& speak harshly of forgiveness.

Tower

after reading Cullen's "From the Dark Tower"
for Lucy Ann Stanton and Gwendolyn Brooks

Ivy and candied yams don't mix.

What must it have been to be the first
black bud beneath ivy-veiled stones.
There you were, breath soft
and quickly obscured. Crossing, climbing
with hoisted ancestor-eyes, making your way to sit at back?
To sit. To sit and listen, your mind whirling, haunted
music popping your veins. And then to hunch
beneath a flicking light. Where was that and
what must it have been?

These certainties:

Yams are not indigenous here.
To sow them one must toil
under rigorous sun. To reap
them backs must bend, arms must reach.
And there you were, sowing and reaping.
And here we are sowing, reaping,
listening for a kindred voice
singing, sanging, sangin' softly, 'chil.

"It Wasn't Not Funny"

Tammi, on *The Real World* (MTV)

Six people in a house more funky and beautiful
than they or I have ever seen, cannot be held accountable
for their empty two-liter bottle behavior. Still, yes

I had expected to be saddened by things whispered when
the cameras were on. I had expected to be shocked by arguments
of youth, when an unwashed dish means dismissal of your Rights,
a misplaced telephone message—the death of your trust in humanity.

I had not expected you, in head rag and torn clothing,
the cameras beseeching some ugliness, in the heat
of an argument, Tammi. Had not expected
when he pulled the blanket from your half-nude body,
your cry of Rape.

My skin doesn't retract easily.
But that day, your mouth made me feel Blacker
than a Poplar, more ghetto than a thousand stolen food stamps,
more defeated than a little girl running from a neighbor's house,
the sound of Dee-Dee's,

"Girl, what's wrong with you—outside with your hair like that!
Don't you ever come out in public with your color showing and
your ass stinking!"
snapping at her heels.

Refrigerator Mouth

for Fe

Her cropped hair reaches and gestates
the humidity to its nappy bosom. Her eyes twinkle
as her tongue tells of a secret, small and really
not a secret at all, just something that made a difference.

Her sister, she says, *of course*, told her boyfriend who then,
like a pussy or a punk, or both, told the man Fe didn't want to know.
That night the man, the one Fe loves,
called and pussyfooted around the matter of where
her daughter was and why he couldn't come over and was generally,
trying to be slick.

Coincidence, she says, *can kiss my ass.*

My sister has a refrigerator mouth.

Once the story is told, we laugh,
and I am back jockeying my desk, I wonder

how many times cucumbers or lettuce
or that stick of butter I couldn't stuff anywhere
without its extruding itself
have fallen from my refrigerator. I wonder too,
if it matters, if I should apologize and to whom.

As on Every Saturday At 12

Shawntay makes her pilgrimage to Greg's Beautification Shop,
which sits on the corner of Florida Avenue and 9th Street,
bopping, writhing, and full of itself;
three floors of plastic bag curls,
wraps, weaves, French rolls—tight and 'bout right.

The hours between noon and dusk are the difference
between good gossip and "child, that's old news."
Still, it's not so bad: tonight, the tithe
bearer's eyes will fall over her—but gently.

Summoned, from the half eaten fish sandwich
and empty soda cans by the new shampoo girl
    (whose butt is worse than unset Jell-O,)
she is told to sit back and relax, *gurl.*

Washed and waiting she peeks at Renee
whose ten inch nails snake around Gold-n-Hot
curlers which spit and hiss and offer salvation.

Dried and ready she is surrendered to The Chair
where sitting still and Goddess-like is worthiness.
Shawntay is. Assured

that if it burns enough, if the hiss is loud enough,
the smell overwhelming enough, the Amen Corner will buzz,
and the buzz will be the word and the word will sound
like: "Oh. My. God. Gurl! That is soooo FLY!"
And she'll be reminded: God is good.

John Edgar Wideman, Apologies . . .

See, we was talkin shit in the bar
u know:
    Whosey was flirtin wit whatchamacallit
    Mr. Man was drunk or damned near
    Somebody's Momma was so ugly the doctor slapped himself
       & quit his job.

We was supposta be workshoppin our poet-tree
& our spirits. Layed back & cool like
color dripping from our mouths
when u walked up
    Amstel Light in hand
asked if u could & then eeled yo-sef into a seat
eyes poppin & lookin like: Come on wit it, young bloods.

But you were the coming of The Word.

So we humbled ourselves
found soap bubblin in our mouths & held it back
wondered if someone didn't have some castor oil in onea them bags
& thought of our mommas.

I have since wondered
what our silence must have been.

Was it like walking into a funeral?
Did the frozen "O's" of our mouths
look like a mother howling?

Was it being sixteen &
walking into a gossip-about-u filled room?

Was it like the silences of Monk
our music hinged
just there & ready to pop?

Was

it

like

that?

55

The First Time I Saw Flo-Jo

for Florence Griffith Joyner (1959–1998)

I almost died when I saw those Nile-nails,
bright as your neon spandex, tacky
& beautiful too.

Flo, girl

you ran like the Boogieman's
worst fear—a Black woman with God
all up in her. Ran so fast you caught
the Boogieman on a tail wind
& boogied his ass back.

> Someone said the Devil
> must have gotten in you
> for you to run like that.

But, the drums of your feet cried
war & our eyes were husks
around your calves; were heavy
with memory; exploded with freedom
each time you burst. We thought: The wind

ain't got a chance. Do it like it ain't been done,
girl. Run like you gotta run, girl. Hotdamn,
look at our sister fly!

& Nail salons got rich,
Spandex was never so chic,
kids poured strawberry Kool-Aid
on dirt, stirred it up & took off
running in ghettos everywhere,
exhaling: jojojojo flojojojo

& in those moments
when you ruptured the wind,
the drums of your feet crying
war, girl, we rallied
we rallied damned
if we didn't rally.

Once Upon a Time

(in Paducah, Springfield, and Pearl)

There was a place called Ameriland,
where the Big Boy on Sunday was holy;
and giant corn stalks met fields, sprouted, prevailed and reached for Jesus;
where rolling clouds were clown-face-white and apples murderous red;
where groups of women gathered round with flour and sugar and cinnamon
clucking over children as necessary as the pies they baked.

And doe-faced children knew only joy in Ameriland,
never heard the wail of Marvin, knew only that the cha-cha
of salsa meant a glass jar at the Piggly Wiggly, slanted eyes—
delivery from the one and only Emerald Garden.

In Ameriland, color was so abundant and so scarce. Plus,
it was only talked about in fierce warning whispers.

It was a big place made up of small towns with names like
Paducah, Springfield, and Pearl
where Mothers and Fathers swathed their children
in soft mounds of cotton when the sun dwindled.
Then, when the children's eyes

were big and not ready for sleep, Mother and Father would tell stories about

Chicanos who inhale tamales, own bodegas, and transform pickup trucks into filthy gyrating machines. About Chicanos named Maria, Xavier, and José, who wield salsa-dipped knives in jail-house brawls. Sometimes they'd tell stories about

Asians who have two toes and belong to Tongs; who shanghai jobs and prosperity; who are a jungle people, evil and formidable because of their cunning which is cloaked in delicate beauty—the most dangerous deception of all. Or Mother and Father would whisper of

Negroes who wear rollers and slippers to the Kentucky Fried and thieve language, creating a labyrinth that is particularly seductive to little Ameriland children who, if they don't eat their carrots and peas, just might be banished to a world of heathenistic clothes and obscene music.

And children in Paducah, Springfield and Pearl closed their eyes somewhere between the middle and end of those tales, snuggled their teddies, echoes of Mother and Father roaming their minds.

Then one day, an Ameriland boy woke to a cold sun and plummeted into a deep abyss. When he fell his piece of Ameriland capsized with a thunderous
Thump.

And then two more little Ameriland boys who had perhaps
heard/seen more than their small eyes could digest
and who had learned the virtues of fire and powder
and trajectory from Grandfather
Ameriland decided they would no longer cry silently and rallied an
explosive explanation. There was another
Thump.

Then, when all the mothers and fathers cross-eyed with suspicion
had taken chaotic notice another of their own pillaged the remaining
fragments until Ameriland exploded with rage and grief red as his
hair. And there was another
Thump.

Meanwhile, the little children, some of which weren't so little,
howled
(upon realizing there were no more clown-faced clouds); and
screeched
(at the bitterness of apples and sugar and cinnamon).

Beseeched: This should not happen Here: (we are not salsa Chicanos).
This should not happen Here: (we are not slanty-eyed Asians).
This should not happen Here: (we are not Kentucky-Fried Negroes).

It was tragic.

And we watched Ameriland explode bit by bit,

looked to the bloody, dusk-filled sky,
found the same decade-old sinister clouds
grinning down on our woe,
heard the soft foreshadowing wail
of Marvin, felt the miasma of our overcast
hovels extending and someone, somewhere
called for Jesus.

Nora

The machine tells
some thing has settled on her.
I hear it tightening, constricting her
vocal cords.

Nora, mother of Nishelle—now two.
Nora, who I can't drag out of her mother's
clawing arms or her boyfriend's pit-bull teeth.

Nora, my shredded billie holiday blue girl.

In these days, when little brown girls
just shedding pigtails or cornrows
find their bodies budding breasts
and growing baby-soft hair
we should all pray—even those who don't believe.

Zawadi

"Gifts"
an inheritance/borrowed poem

I have heard you are fussy
keeping your daddy and momma on point
your small mouth already forming itself
around the vowels of revolution.

Your momma tells that you
came out on someone else's
terms. I imagined you thinking:
"I'ma remember this shit
and I'll be back."

I have seen your picture at two weeks old,
brow already furrowed.

> *Here are some names you should know:*
> *alicedorothyj.californiaishmaelamirilucillemargaretlangstonzora.*

Zawadi, when you were born
girl-children, their baby-soft hair
just budding, were propagating.
When you were born we were killing ourselves.

63

When you were born I shouted
and stomped and danced
threw up my hands in a mighty "Hallelujah!"

Girl, when you're old enough,
I'll whisper you Toni Cade's Goldie Locks:
> ". . . a little white child broke into some folk's house
> —now what do we call people who break into other people's houses?
> And so now this little white burglar child went inside and messed up
>   the folk's house.
> —now what do we call people who mess up other people's houses?
> And so now this little white burglar vandal child didn't stop there . . ."

And, there are stories of your father I'll tell:
the time he cussed out so and so;
how many of us he gently pushed
into the shifting of words; how revolution begins.

> *Here are some names you should know:*
> *sonianikkihakintozakejimmyyusefgwenmayarichardralphtonitoni*

Zawadi, there is so much to say. For now:
I wish you Kool-Aid summers.
I wish you the O'Jays and HoolaHoops.
I wish you cornrows and beads and Big Wheels.
I wish you Black tomorrows
and pray they fall on you
gently, girl.

oo-bop-she-bam

In Search of Aunt Jemima

I have sailed the south rivers of China and prayed to hillside Buddahs.
I've lived in Salamanca, Cuernavaca, Misawa, and Madrid. Have stood
upon the anointed sands of Egypt and found my soul in their grains.

I've read more fiction, nonfiction, biographies, poetry, magazines,
essays, and bullshit than imaginable, possible, or even practical. I am
beyond well read, am somewhat of a bibliophile. Still, I'm gawked at
by white girls on subways who want to know why and how I'm
reading T. S. Eliot.

I've shopped Hong Kong and Bangkok out in heat so hot the trees
were looking for shade—I was the hottest thing around. I'm followed
in corner stores, grocery stores, any store.

I can issue you insults in German, Spanish, and a little Japanese.
I'm still greeted by wannabe-hip white boys in half-assed ghettoese.
I've been 250 pounds, 150 pounds and have lived and loved
every pound in between. I am still restricted by Nell Carter images of me.

I've eaten rabbit in Rome, paella in Barcelona, couscous in Morocco,
and am seated at the worst table by mentally challenged Maitre'd's
who think my big ass is there for coffee.

I am still passed up by cabs
passed over for jobs
ignored by politicians
guilty before innocent
Black before human.
And I'm expected to know Snoop Dog's latest hit
Mike's latest scandal
I'm expected to believe in O.J.'s innocence.
And I am still expected to walk white babies up and down 92nd street
as I nurse them, sing a hymn and dance a jig.

Sorry, not this sista, sista-girl, miss boo, miss it, miss thang, honey,
honey-child, girl, girlfriend.

See, I am not your militant right-on sista wearing dashikis and 'fros with
my fist in the air spouting Black Power while smoking weed,
burning incense and making love to Shaka—formally known as Tyrone.

I am not your high-yellow saditty college girl flaunting Gucci bags
and Armani suits driving
an alabaster colored Beemer with tinted windows and A.K.A.
    symbols rimming my license plate.

I am not your three-babies-by-fifteen, green dragon lady press on
nails whose rambunctious ass is stuffed into too tight lycra with a
lollipop hanging out the side of my mouf and a piece of hair
caught in a rubberband stuck to the top of my head.

I am not your Timberland, Tommy Hilfiger,
10K hollow-hoop wearin
gangsta rappin
crack dealin
blunt smokin
bandanna wearin
Bitch named Poochie.

I am not your conscience clearer.
I am not your convenient Black friend.
Notyourprototypenotyoursellout 'cuz
massa and the big house is too good.

I am not your Aunt Jemima.

In my (8,957) days of Black womanhood I've learned this:
Be careful of what you say
of what you think
of what you do
because you never know

who you're talking to.

Ode of the Hoodoo Woman

I.

If you let me lie I will sing you
a Hoodoo Woman's Song. Loud. Fierce.

Would make the drums of my voice
the voice of your mother
and hers lulling you into forgiveness Baby, Sugar, Sweetness.

If you let me lie I will dance the dance of disease
rampant and faceless. The dance of men
who make babies and broken hearts
Could make their weaknesses my rhythm.

Let me cast you a spell, wish myself into your dreams, conjured;
swinging these rounded hips, chanting some magic words, making myself
not fat but plump; not cute but beautiful, perhaps even exotic.
Let me brew a blaming stew a commercial stock my base.
Let me chant until my throat grows hoarse.
Let me cast myself out of this sin. Let me get down
on dirtied knees. Let me pray. Let me call
on DNA—my God and Antichrist.

II.

There is no magic spell
binding. No Hoodoo.
Only my feet, wide and flat,
hitting the ground, carrying me to work then home.

No conjuring 'cept the songs of my father—jazzy-soft and
the touches of mother—pulling on coats, tying on shoes, combing
my hair into niceties. These are the only spells I know.

Most days, the sun out
or the clouds tight and gnarled, here,
not sexy, not slim, I stand. Peeling
off the excess excuses like armor;
peeling the tired/tried rhythms of fierceness;
peeling, like a potato, until I am glistening and clammy.

Not Hoodoo Woman.
Not Mamma Woman.
Not Strong Independent Woman.
Not Too Much of a Woman.
Only raw, small, and afraid.

III. Coda

There is too much talk about the weather.

For now, I will say
it was my father's death
coming like molasses from a jar:
that winter for the first time a cold car,
unshoveled snow.

And it was my high school boyfriend
who may have never learned being a man means
not dumping your girlfriend on Prom eve.

I could leave it with a list of names:
Grump the Simple, or Leo the Gigolo, or Wil the Decimator,
or Melvin or Michael or Anthony.

Or I could change tracks:
It was hugging Scott, his AIDS body slim and brittle,
unlike his smile.

I might say:
Only children have a hard time learning compromise,
the media is too full of beautifully created women,
the women's movement was before my time,
the Black brown bruthas are locked up or straying
or not accessible.

On good days, it is a culmination,
a slow heaping on of reasons
like dirty dishes or garbage dumps,
that grows until it is repugnant and easily ignored.

"Breeze Driftin' On By

You know how I feel . . ."
Nina Simone

To the Chilean woman-poet who said there are no political-poets
    writing in North America except for old white women.

To the man who asked the side of my face
    for a cigarette.

To the woman in California who pays drug-addicted women
    to self-sterilize for a rate of two hundred dollars.

To the man who assumed I could tell him
    where to cop some ganja.

To the student who shrouded his comparison of Black peoples
    to marginalized Modernists.

To the classmates who did not speak
    up or out.

To the romantic white girl-child who wants to be Black
    if only not to be white.

To the politicians who thought to offer pittance to those held
  hostage in internment camps.

To the politicians who thought to offer no pittance to
  families of expunged Africans.

To the folk who voted for those politicians.

To those people. To them. To all
of them who don't know
how
or why
or what it is to be

a breeze driftin'.

Here.

I gift you this. I bequeath.
I bequest one moment on any street when eyes meet.
I give you that single second. My arms are wider, stronger.
I offer you it, hear. Here. Here.

Notes

Johnny: This poem refers to a song, also titled "Johnny," recorded by Aretha Franklin ("Sweet Bitter Love" 1982).

Collard Folk: "Mudia" represents the phonetic combination of "My" and "Dear." Other variations are "Mydear" and "Mudear." These representations are most commonly found in southern regions of the the United States.

Dré: The italicized texts were exerpted from "I Love Lord," recorded by Whitney Houston ("The Preacher's Wife" 1996).

Tower: Lucy Ann Stanton was the first Black woman to receive a college degree (1850, Oberlin). Gwendolyn Brooks was the first Black woman to receive a Pulitzer Prize (1950, *Annie Allen*).

The First Time I Saw Flo-Jo: After the sudden death of Olympic athlete Florence Griffith Joyner in 1998, a short-lived controversy ensued about her alleged use of steroids. It was later proven that she did not use drugs.

Once Upon A Time (In Paducah, Springfield, and Pearl): The factual events to which the poem refers are a combination of four incidents which took place in Springfield, Ore.; Jonesboro, Ark.; West Paducah, Ky.; and Pearl, Mississippi.

Zawadi: The paraphrased version of Goldie Locks was taken from a video in which novelist Toni Cade Bambara told the story to a group of children in a book shop.

Ode of the Hoodoo Woman: The phrase, "There is too much talk about the weather" is original to poet/professor Ruth Danon.

Breeze Driftin' On By: The title and epigram were both excerpted from "Feeling Good," recorded by Nina Simone ("Compact Jazz: Nina Simone" 1989).

Crystal Williams, a native of Detroit, Michigan, holds a B.A. from NYU and a M.F.A. from Cornell University. Her work has been published in journals/anthologies such as *Icarus, The Potomac Review, Spectrum, WV, American Poetry: The Next Generation, Catch the Fire, Poetry Nation,* and *Children of the Dream.* She was a member of the 1995 Nuyorican Poets Café National Slam Team. *Kin* is her first book.